Grand Teton
Magazine Mountain
Mauna Kea
Mount Elbert
Mount McKinley

Mount Mitchell
Mount Rainier
Mount Saint Elias
Mount Washington
Mount Whitney

AMERICA'S TOP 10 MOUNTAINS

By
Jenny Tesar

Published by Blackbirch Press, Inc.
260 Amity Road
Woodbridge, CT 06525

©1998 Blackbirch Press, Inc.
First Edition

Printed in the USA

10 9 8 7 6 5 4 3 2 1

Library of Congress Cataloging-in-Publication Data

Tesar, Jenny E.
    America's top 10 mountains / by Jenny Tesar.
        p. cm.—(America's top 10)
    Includes bibliographical references and index.
    Summary: Discusses ten of America's most unique mountains: Grand Teton, Magazine
Mountain, Mauna Kea, Mount Elbert, Mount McKinley, Mount Mitchell, Mount Rainier,
Mount Saint Elias, Mount Washington, and Mount Whitney.
    ISBN 1-56711-196-3 (lib. bdg. : alk. paper)
    1. Mountains—United States—Juvenile literature. [1. Mountains] I. Title. II. Series.
GB525.T47   1998   97–3638
551.43'2—dc21   CIP
                                                                              AC

BLACKBIRCH PRESS, INC.
WOODBRIDGE, CONNECTICUT

AMERICA'S TOP

10

MOUNTAINS

★ Grand
Teton

MT

ID

SD

WY

NE

UT

CO

Grand Teton

Magnificent Grand Teton towers over Wyoming's Teton Range and the surrounding countryside. Its jagged peak and sheer walls can be seen 100 miles away. The most stunning views of this mountain are from the eastern base of the range.

The Tetons began forming about 9 million years ago, which makes them some of the youngest mountains in America. They are called "fault-block" mountains because they were pushed up from the earth's crust by a series of earthquakes. The fault line lies along the eastern base of the range, and this side of the mountain rises sharply. Grand Teton's eastern slope rises about 7,000 feet from the valley below.

At an elevation of 13,770 feet above sea level, Grand Teton is separated from its neighbor, Middle Teton, by a pass called Lower Saddle. At 13,200 feet, not far from Grand Teton's summit, a smaller pass called Upper Saddle separates the mountain's main peak from a smaller peak to the west. Just above Upper Saddle is a narrow ledge named the Crawl. Many adventurous people who climb Grand Teton wriggle along this ledge on their stomachs!

Grand Teton's main peak is rough and almost pointed. It is a very windy spot. Although a lot of snow falls on the peak, most of the snow is blown away by the wind.

At lower altitudes, Grand Teton is covered by forests. Pines, firs, and aspen are the dominant trees. Tree line—the point above which it is too cold for trees—is at 10,000 feet.

Name: From French words meaning "large breast"
Height: 13,770 feet above sea level
Location: Wyoming
Mountain range: The Teton Range, part of the American section of the Rocky Mountains
Park: Grand Teton National Park
Earliest recorded climb to the summit: By William O. Owen and 3 other men in 1898
Wildlife: Bald eagle, bighorn sheep, elk, marmot, moose, mule deer, pronghorn antelope
Fun fact: Native Americans called the Teton Range Teewinot, which means "many pinnacles."

Opposite page:
Grand Teton is the highest peak in the Teton Range.

AMERICA'S TOP

10

MOUNTAINS

MO

OK

Magazine
Mountain

TN

AR

TX

MS

LA

Magazine Mountain

Most of the central United States consists of vast, grassy plains of flat or gently rolling land. But in the south-central part of the country are the Ozark Mountains. They stretch across northern Arkansas and southern Missouri and include parts of Oklahoma and Kansas. The tallest of the Ozarks is Magazine Mountain. Although this is the highest point between the Appalachian Mountains, to the east, and the Rocky Mountains, to the west, Magazine Mountain rises only 2,753 feet above sea level. In a sense, the Ozarks aren't really mountains. They were formed from a plateau that rose up from the surrounding land—geologists say this land was "uplifted." Rivers eroded some areas of the plateau more than others, creating valleys and "mountains."

Magazine Mountain sits between two river valleys: the Arkansas River valley to the north, and the Petit Jean River valley to the south. A scenic road crosses the mountain from north to south. The top of Magazine Mountain is mostly flat. Travelers can park their cars there, and then take a short walk up to Signal Hill, the mountain's peak.

The mountain is covered by forest. Pine, oak, and hickory are the most common trees. The oak and hickory trees on the mountaintop are much smaller than those on the slopes, even though many are as old—or older. The trees are stunted because the mountaintop's climate is harsh. Dogwood trees also grow on Magazine Mountain, and in spring they are covered with blossoms.

Name: Believed to be named for its resemblance to a magazine—a fort-like building where goods are stored

Height: 2,753 feet above sea level

Location: Arkansas

Mountain range: Boston Mountains, part of the Ozarks

Park: Ozark National Forest

Average annual snowfall: Several inches

Wildlife: Armadillo, barred owl, black bear, great horned owl, opossum, raccoon, red-tailed hawk, squirrel, white-tailed deer

Fun fact: The Diana butterfly and a small snail called the Magazine Mountain shagreen can be found only on Magazine Mountain.

Opposite page:
Many of the trees on Magazine Mountain turn golden in the fall.

AMERICA'S TOP
10
MOUNTAINS

Mauna
Kea

HI

Mauna Kea

★ ★ ★ ★ ★ ★ ★ ★ ★ ★ ★ ★ ★ ★ ★ ★ ★

High above the town of Hilo, on the island of Hawaii, is Mauna Kea. This volcano rises 13,796 feet above sea level. It is the highest mountain in the world if it is measured from its base on the ocean floor, rather than at sea level. Mauna Kea began forming when hot liquid rock, called lava, poured out of cracks on the Pacific Ocean floor. Gradually, over hundreds of thousands of years, the lava accumulated, and the mountain grew. It broke through the surface of the water and kept rising. From its base, Mauna Kea measures 33,500 feet high!

The road leading to the top of Mauna Kea passes through many different environments. On the mountain's lower slopes are sugar-cane fields and grasslands. Further up the slope, more lava is visible. It comes in many colors—black, brown, red, and silver—and in many shapes. Plants have broken down the older lava, creating soil. Ferns and ohia bushes covered with red blossoms decorate the landscape. Closer to the summit, there are no plants. Some of the wildlife on Mauna Kea are found nowhere else in the world. One, a bird called the palila, lives at least 6,000 feet above sea level.

At 13,020 feet lies Lake Waiau—the third-highest lake in the United States. The summit of Mauna Kea provides spectacular views across the island of Hawaii toward the Pacific Ocean. The air on the summit is very clear, and many telescopes have been placed there. The Mauna Kea Observatory Complex includes two Keck telescopes—the largest telescopes ever built.

Name: From Hawaiian words meaning "white mountain"
Height: 13,796 feet above sea level
Location: Hawaii
Mountain range: None
Parks: Pohakuloa State Park, State Science Reserve Area
Wildlife: Hawaiian goose, mouflon sheep, pheasant, wild pig
Fun fact: In 1996, an astronomer using the Mauna Kea Observatory discovered the first brown dwarf, an object in outer space that is bigger than a planet but not quite a star.

Opposite page:
Mauna Kea can be seen clearly from the lava-covered base of Mauna Loa, which is another volcano.

AMERICA'S TOP

10

MOUNTAINS

	WY		NE
UT			
	CO		
	★ **Mount Elbert**		KS
AZ			
	NM		OK

Mount Elbert

★ ★ ★ ★ ★ ★ ★ ★ ★ ★ ★ ★ ★ ★ ★ ★ ★

Mount Elbert, located in central Colorado, is the highest peak in the American part of the Rocky Mountains, which also extend north into Canada. It is a fairly easy mountain to climb. Three trails lead to the summit, which is 14,433 feet above sea level.

The summit of Mount Elbert is large and broad. Its height makes weather harsh—it is usually very windy on top of the mountain. Below, patches of snow sometimes remain on the ground even in warm weather. Every so often, snow falls in the middle of summer!

Mount Elbert is part of the Sawatch Mountains, the tallest of the many ranges that make up the Rockies. This range runs along the Continental Divide—the "backbone of America." All the rivers on the west side of this imaginary line flow toward the Pacific Ocean. Those on the east side flow toward the Gulf of Mexico and the Atlantic Ocean. Mount Elbert is just to the east of the Continental Divide. The streams that originate on the mountain, such as Elbert Creek and Bartlett Gulch, eventually empty into the Arkansas River. This river—one of America's longest—flows into the Mississippi, which empties into the Gulf of Mexico.

The lower elevations of Mount Elbert are covered by forest. Lodgepole pine, Engelmann spruce, and aspen are the most common trees there. The tree line is at an elevation of between 11,000 and 12,000 feet. Above that, large areas are filled with alpine wildflowers.

Name: Honors Samuel H. Elbert, a public official in Colorado during the 19th century.
Height: 14,433 feet above sea level
Location: Colorado
Mountain range: Sawatch Mountains (part of the American Rockies)
Park: San Isabel National Forest
Wildlife: Badger, deer, eagle, elk, fox, goshawk, porcupine, ptarmigan, weasel
Fun fact: The Sawatch range includes 15 mountains that are 14,000 feet or more in height, which is a record for the United States.

Opposite page:
Nestled in the American Rockies, Mount Elbert creates a high point.

AMERICA'S TOP

10

MOUNTAINS

AK

CANADA

Mount
McKinley

Mount McKinley

★ ★ ★ ★ ★ ★ ★ ★ ★ ★ ★ ★ ★ ★ ★ ★

Alaska's Mount McKinley (known in Alaska as Denali) is America's highest mountain. South Peak, the taller of its twin peaks, soars 20,320 feet above sea level. Two miles away is North Peak, which is somewhat lower. Separating the peaks is Denali Pass.

Mount McKinley is part of the Alaska Range. These mountains are called "uplift mountains." They began forming about 60 million years ago when two plates, or pieces, of the earth's crust collided. This forced huge masses of rock upward. About 2 million years ago, new plate collisions started, which are still occurring, thrusting the Alaska Range even higher.

Since the Alaska Range first began taking shape, the mountains have been eroded by running water, such as streams. Mount McKinley is composed mainly of granite—a hard rock that erodes more slowly than other kinds of rock. For this reason, the mountain stands more than 3 miles above the surrounding land.

Mount McKinley is so high that on clear days it can be seen more than 100 miles away. Most of the time, however, it is hidden from view by fog and clouds. Severe storms in the area, sometimes lasting for weeks, are common.

Snow and ice cover Mount McKinley year-round. No one knows exactly how much snow falls on the summit, however, because weather equipment cannot function in the high winds at the top. At the base of the mountain, which is 7,200 feet above sea level, as much as 8 feet of snow may fall in a single snowstorm.

Name: Honors William McKinley, 25th president of the United States
Height: 20,320 feet above sea level
Location: Alaska
Mountain range: Alaska Range
Park: Denali National Park
Earliest recorded climb to the summit: By Hudson Stuck, Walter Harper, Harry Karstens, and Robert Tatum in 1913
Wildlife: Bald eagle, black bear, finch, raven
Fun fact: Aleuts—natives of Alaska—named this mountain Denali, "the high one."

Opposite page:
A clear view of Mount McKinley's peak is a rare sight.

AMERICA'S TOP

10

MOUNTAINS

KY

WV

VA

TN

Mount
Mitchell

NC

GA

SC

Atlantic Ocean

Mount Mitchell

★ ★ ★ ★ ★ ★ ★ ★ ★ ★ ★ ★ ★ ★ ★ ★ ★

Mount Mitchell is the tallest mountain east of the Mississippi River. It is located in the Black Mountains of western North Carolina. These mountains are named after the dark green forests that cover their summits, making the mountains appear black.

The Black Mountains are the highest section of the Blue Ridge Mountains, which are famous for their beauty. In spring and early summer, mountain laurel, azalea, and masses of rhododendron are in bloom. The Blue Ridge is part of the Appalachians, a chain of mountain ranges that is about 1,500 miles long. It runs parallel to the Atlantic Ocean, from Canada to Alabama.

The Appalachians are called "folded mountains." They were formed when pressure under the earth's surface pushed the rock layers upward, causing them to fold over. Long ago, the Appalachians were much higher than they are today. For millions of years, they have been worn down (eroded) by glacial action and running water.

On the summit of Mount Mitchell is a gray stone tower. It was built in memory of Elisha Mitchell, for whom the mountain is named. When the sky is clear, there are spectacular views from the summit, although the mountain is often blanketed by clouds and fog.

Red spruce and Fraser fir are the most common trees in the dense forests of Mount Mitchell. Many of these trees are covered with small organisms called "lichens," which come in many shapes. Some cling like barnacles to tree trunks. Others hang from branches in thread-like masses.

Name: Honors Elisha Mitchell, who measured the mountain's height in 1835
Height: 6,684 feet above sea level
Location: North Carolina
Mountain range: Black Mountains—part of the Blue Ridge Mountains, in the Appalachian mountain range
Parks: Mount Mitchell State Park and Pisgah National Forest
Average annual snowfall: About 104 inches
Wildlife: Black bear, bobcat, deer, grouse, raven, squirrel, white-tailed deer
Fun fact: During the Ice Age that ended about 11,000 years ago, saber-toothed tigers and mastodons roamed the Black Mountains.

Opposite page:
Like other mountains in the Appalachian range, Mount Mitchell has been eroded by glaciers.

AMERICA'S TOP

10

MOUNTAINS

CANADA

★ Mount
Rainier   WA

OR   ID

Mount Rainier

★ ★ ★ ★ ★ ★ ★ ★ ★ ★ ★ ★ ★ ★ ★ ★ ★ ★ ★

Mount Rainier is one of America's most beautiful mountains. Located near Seattle, Washington, it is the highest mountain in the Cascade Range. When the sky is clear, Mount Rainier's snow-covered peak can be seen for hundreds of miles in all directions.

The mountain is actually a volcano that started forming about 1 million years ago. It grew larger and larger as layer after layer of molten rock spouted from an opening in the earth's crust. Mount Rainier's last major eruptions occurred about 2,000 years ago, but smaller ones took place within the past 200 years. Today, steam rises from the 2 craters on the summit, which suggests that the volcano may erupt again.

The upper slopes of Mount Rainier are covered with snow and ice year-round. The summit is broad and rounded and has 3 peaks. Columbia Crest is the highest. The other 2 are Liberty Cap and Point Success.

Many glaciers have formed on the mountain. The longest is Carbon Glacier. The largest is Emmons Glacier. One of the fastest moving is Nisqually Glacier. As the glaciers move, they erode the underlying rock, changing the shape of the mountain. In warm weather, huge masses of ice and snow break off from glaciers and tumble down the mountainside. On the lower slopes of Mount Rainier are meadows filled with colorful wildflowers in spring and summer. Below the tree line—at about 6,000 feet—are forests of tall evergreens. The forests and surrounding foothills are often covered by fog.

Name: Given by British navigator George Vancouver in honor of his friend, British Rear Admiral Peter Rainier

Height: 14,410 feet above sea level

Location: Washington

Mountain range: Cascade Range

Park: Mount Rainier National Park

Average annual snowfall: More than 45 feet

Earliest recorded climb to the summit: By Hazard Stevens and Philemon Beecher Van Trump in 1870

Wildlife: Chipmunk, horned lark, marmot, mountain goat, pika, ptarmigan, rosy finch, squirrel, water pipit

Fun fact: Native Americans called this mountain Tahoma, which means "the mountain that was God."

Opposite page:
Mount Rainier stands on a flat plateau, separated from other peaks in the Cascade Range.

AMERICA'S TOP

10

MOUNTAINS

AK Mount Saint Elias CANADA

Mount Saint Elias

★ ★ ★ ★ ★ ★ ★ ★ ★ ★ ★ ★ ★ ★ ★ ★ ★ ★ ★ ★

The second-highest peak in the United States is Mount Saint Elias, which lies on the border between Alaska and Canada, near the Gulf of Alaska. Emptying into the gulf is Icy Bay, named for the many icebergs that float in its waters. These giant chunks of ice break off, or calve, from glaciers on Mount Saint Elias and other mountains in the Saint Elias range. When a chunk of ice calves and falls into the water, it makes a thunderous splash.

The largest glacier in the region is the vast Malaspina Glacier, along the southern base of the mountain. This glacier is larger than the state of Rhode Island! Smaller glaciers that are moving down the sides of Saint Elias and neighboring mountains feed into Malaspina Glacier.

The Saint Elias Mountains are called "uplift mountains" because they formed when two plates of the earth's crust collided. Masses of rock were forced upward, creating the mountains.

Mount Saint Elias is comparatively young. It has steep cliffs and jagged peaks that have not yet been worn down by erosion. Most of Mount Saint Elias is covered with snow year-round. This surface snow often hides deep crevasses, or narrow openings, which can be death traps for careless climbers. Another danger is avalanches—masses of snow, ice, and other materials that tumble swiftly down a mountainside. The Saint Elias Mountains have some of the worst weather in the world. Huge storms sweep in from the Pacific Ocean, bringing violent winds and heavy snowfall.

Name: Honors a Catholic saint
Height: 18,008 feet above sea level
Location: Alaska
Mountain range: Saint Elias Mountains
Park: Wrangell–Saint Elias National Park
Earliest recorded climb to the summit: By a group led by Prince Luigi Amedeo of Savoy, Duke of the Abruzzi, in 1897
Wildlife: Caribou, Dall sheep, eagle, hawk, Steller jay, wolf
Fun fact: Wrangell–Saint Elias National Park is America's largest national park. It is more than 3 times as big as Yellowstone National Park.

Opposite page:
The snow-covered peak of the mountain rises into the clouds.

AMERICA'S TOP

10

MOUNTAINS

CANADA

ME

VT

Mount
Washington

NH

Atlantic
Ocean

NY

MA

★ ★ ★ ★ ★ ★ ★ ★ ★ ★ ★ ★ ★ ★ ★ ★ ★ ★

Mount Washington

At 6,288 feet above sea level, Mount Washington is the highest mountain in New England. It is part of the northern Appalachians.

Mount Washington is an old mountain that was formed more than 350 million years ago. When it was young, it was much higher than it is today. Over hundreds of millions of years, however, the mountain has been worn down by erosion. Many of its features were created by the movement of glaciers that once covered its slopes. These large "rivers" of ice carved several enormous, bowl-shaped valleys called "cirques" into the sides of the mountain. The last glaciers melted about 12,000 years ago.

Forests cover Mount Washington's slopes to an elevation of about 3,300 feet above sea level. Above the tree line is tundra, where only mosses, grasses, and other low-growing plants can survive. The layer of soil on the tundra is thin, and the summer growing season is short. In spite of these harsh conditions, many small, beautiful flowering plants are found among the rocks.

The summit of Mount Washington is famous for its howling winds. In winter, they often blow at a speed of 200 miles per hour. In summer, it is fairly easy to climb to the top, where there is a weather station and an observation center. One of the most interesting ways to reach the summit is on the Mount Washington Cog Railway, which has been operating since 1869. It takes the railway 3 hours to climb to the top of the mountain and then return to the base.

Name: Honors George Washington, first president of the United States

Height: 6,288 feet above sea level

Location: New Hampshire

Mountain range: Presidential Range in the White Mountains, which are part of the Appalachians

Park: Most of the mountain is in White Mountain National Forest.

Average annual snowfall: 255 inches

Earliest recorded climb to the summit: By Darby Field and 2 others in 1642

Wildlife: Beaver, black bear, crow, deer, fox, hawk, moose, raccoon, raven

Fun fact: The first passenger vehicle reached the summit in 1861. It was a stagecoach drawn by 8 horses.

Opposite page:
The sugar maple trees on the lower slopes of Mount Washington turn red in the fall.

AMERICA'S TOP

10

MOUNTAINS

OR
ID
CA
NV
UT
Mount
Whitney
Pacific Ocean
AZ
MEXICO

Mount Whitney

America's tallest mountain outside Alaska is Mount Whitney. It is part of a great mountain range called the Sierra Nevada, Spanish for "snowy, saw-toothed mountain range." The Sierra Nevada range is located along the eastern border of California. The mountains in this range are called "fault-block mountains" because they formed along a fault, or crack, in the earth's crust. Millions of years ago, earthquakes along the fault line lifted and tilted a block of rock hundreds of miles long that became the Sierra Nevada. The mountain slopes facing the fault—the eastern side of the range—rise almost straight up. The eastern side of Mount Whitney rises abruptly from Owens Valley for about 11,000 feet. The western side slopes much more gradually.

Mount Whitney is in the southern part of the Sierra Nevada, near Death Valley. It is not particularly distinctive when viewed from afar. Up close, however, Mount Whitney is very dramatic, because it rises so abruptly. Its beauty may explain why it is the most frequently climbed mountain in the Sierra Nevada.

The lower slopes of the mountain are covered with evergreen forests. Only small plants survive above the tree line, at about 11,000 feet. Even at the summit, however—14,494 feet above sea level—flowering plants have taken root. The summit is nearly flat and is covered with several acres of large rocks. An average of 150 to 200 inches of snow fall there each year. Although the mountain is not covered with snow year-round, it has several glaciers and permanent snowfields.

Name: Honors Josiah D. Whitney, who helped found the California Geological Survey in 1860

Height: 14,494 feet above sea level

Location: California

Mountain range: Sierra Nevada

Park: Sequoia and Kings Canyon National Park

Earliest recorded climb to the summit: By Charles D. Begole, Albert H. Johnson, and John Lucas in 1873

Wildlife: Deer, marmot, pica, rosy finch, squirrel, vole

Fun fact: Begole, Johnson, and Lucas climbed Mount Whitney because they wanted to escape the hot weather at lower elevations.

Opposite page: Mount Whitney is the tallest American mountain outside Alaska.

America's Top 10 Mountains are not necessarily the tallest in America. Each of them is distinctive, however, and the tallest in its range. Below is a list of America's highest points.

Highest Point in Each State

State, Highest Point, *Elevation (no. of feet above sea level)*

Alabama, Cheaha Mountain, *2,405*

Alaska, Mount McKinley, *20,320*

Arizona, Humphreys Peak, *12,633*

Arkansas, Magazine Mountain, *2,753*

California, Mount Whitney, *14,494*

Colorado, Mount Elbert, *14,433*

Connecticut, Mount Frissell, *2,380*

Delaware, Ebright Road— New Castle County, *442*

Florida, unnamed rise in Walton County, *345*

Georgia, Brasstown Bald, *4,784*

Hawaii, Mauna Kea, *13,796*

Idaho, Borah Peak, *12,662*

Illinois, Charles Mound, *1,235*

Indiana, Franklin Township, *1,257*

Iowa, unnamed rise in Osceola County, *1,670*

Kansas, Mount Sunflower, *4,039*

Kentucky, Black Mountain, *4,139*

Louisiana, Driskill Mountain, *535*

Maine, Mount Katahdin, *5,267*

Maryland, Backbone Mountain, *3,360*

Massachusetts, Mount Greylock, *3,487*

Michigan, Mount Arvon, *1,979*

Minnesota, Eagle Mountain, *2,301*

Mississippi, Woodall Mountain, *806*

Missouri, Taum Sauk Mountain, *1,772*

Montana, Granite Peak, *12,799*

Nebraska, unnamed rise in Johnson Township, *5,426*

Nevada, Boundary Peak, *13,140*

New Hampshire, Mount Washington, *6,288*

New Jersey, High Point, *1,803*

New Mexico, Wheeler Peak, *13,161*

New York, Mount Marcy, *5,344*

North Carolina, Mount Mitchell, *6,684*

North Dakota, White Butte, *3,506*

Ohio, Campbell Hill, *1,549*

Oklahoma, Black Mesa, *4,973*

Oregon, Mount Hood, *11,239*

Pennsylvania, Mount Davis, *3,213*

Rhode Island, Jerimoth Hill, *812*

South Carolina, Sassafras Mountain, *3,560*

South Dakota, Harney Peak, *7,242*

Tennessee, Clingmans Dome, *6,643*

Texas, Guadalupe Peak, *8,749*

Utah, Kings Peak, *13,528*

Vermont, Mount Mansfield, *4,393*

Virginia, Mount Rogers, *5,729*

Washington, Mount Rainier, *14,410*

West Virginia, Spruce Knob, *4,861*

Wisconsin, Timms Hill, *1,951*

Wyoming, Gannett Peak, *13,804*

Glossary

cirque A bowl-shaped valley.

crust The outer layer of the earth.

deciduous trees Trees that shed their leaves in autumn.

earthquake A sudden shaking of the earth's crust.

elevation Distance above sea level.

erode To wear away. Running water erodes rock and soil particles from a mountain.

evergreen trees Trees that have leaves year-round.

fault A crack or break in the earth's crust along which movement occurs.

glacier A large mass of moving ice and snow.

range A group of mountains.

sea level The average level of the surface of the world's oceans. Sea level is the starting point for measuring the elevation of mountains.

summit The top of a mountain.

tree line The area on a mountain above which trees rarely grow.

tundra An area above the tree line on mountains and in arctic regions, where the soil beneath the top layer is permanently frozen.

Further Reading

Arvetis, Chris and Carole Palmer. *Mountains.* Skokie, IL: Rand McNalley & Co., 1993.

Barnes-Svarney, Patricia L. *Born of Heat and Pressure: Mountains and Metamorphic Rocks.* Springfield, NJ: Enslow, 1991.

Bradley, Catherine. *Life in the Mountains.* New York: Scholastic, Inc., 1993.

Bramwell, Martyn. *Mountains.* New York: Franklin Watts, 1994.

Collinson, Allan. *Mountains.* Morristown, NJ: Silver Burdett, 1992.

Knapp, Brian. *Volcano.* Chatham, NJ: Raintree Steck-Vaughn, 1990.

Lauber, Patricia. *Volcanoes and Earthquakes.* New York: Scholastic, Inc., 1991.

Mariner, Tom. *Mountains.* Tarrytown, NY: Marshall Cavendish, 1990.

Steele, Philip. *Mountains.* Morristown, NJ: Silver Burdett, 1991.

Tilling, Robert I. *Born of Fire: Volcanoes and Igneous Rocks.* Springfield, NJ: Enslow, 1991.

Where to Get On-Line Information

Grand Teton	http://www.nps.gov/grte
Mauna Kea	http://www.book.uci.edu/Books/Moon/mauna_kea.html
Mount McKinley	http://www.nps.gov/dena
Mount Rainier	http://www.ohwy.com/wa/m/mtrainnp.htm
Mount Saint Elias	http://www.nps.gov/wrst
Mount Washington	http://www.whitemtn.org/tour.html
Mount Whitney	http://www.nps.gov/seki/whitney.htm

Index

Photo Credits

Cover and page 2: James P. Blair/National Geographic Image Collection; cover and page 4: Robyn Horn/Arkansas Department of Parks and Tourism; cover and page 6: ©Rick Golt/Photo Researchers; cover and page 8: ©Barbara Mallette/Leadville Picture Company; cover and page 10: Alaska Division of Tourism; cover and page 12: North Carolina Travel and Tourism; cover and page 14: PhotoDisc, Inc.; cover and page 16: Alaska Division of Tourism/NPS/David Cohen; cover and page 18: Dick Hamilton Photo ©White Mountain News Bureau/State of New Hampshire Tourism; cover and page 20: ©Jane Dove Juneau.